GW00492978

REBECCA WINTER

Our Baby

The First Year

A KEEPSAKE ALBUM

LION
Giftlines

This edition copyright © 1998 Lion Publishing
Illustrations copyright © 1998 Linda Baker-Smith

The author and artist have asserted their moral rights
to be identified as the author and artist of this work

Published by
Lion Publishing plc
Sandy Lane West, Oxford, England
ISBN 0 7459 3981 3

First edition 1998
10 9 8 7 6 5 4 3 2 1 0

All rights reserved

A catalogue record for this book is
available from the British Library

Acknowledgments
Cover photograph by Leonard Smith, Lens Ideas.
The Bible quotation from Psalm 67 is taken from The New Revised Standard Version
of the Bible, Anglicized Edition, copyright © 1989, 1995 by the Division of Christian
Education of the National Council of the Churches of Christ in the United States of
America, and is used by permission. All rights reserved.
All other Bible quotations are taken from the *Good News Bible* published by The
Bible Societies/HarperCollins Publishers Ltd, UK © American Bible Society, 1966,
1971, 1976, 1992.
Extract from the *Alternative Service Book 1980* is copyright © The Central Board of
Finance of the Church of England and is reproduced by permission.
The Laurie Lee quote is taken from *I Can't Stay Long* by Laurie Lee (Penguin Books,
1977) copyright © Laurie Lee, 1975. Reproduced by permission of Penguin Books.

Printed and bound in Malaysia

Introduction

'Before you know it she'll be at school,' a friend said, looking at my two-day-old daughter. At the time I thought it was a ridiculous thing to say: I couldn't even think a week ahead, let alone five years! But now, only a year later, I realize the truth of those words. Children grow up literally before your eyes.

Only a month or so after being born a baby can smile and can quickly recognize voices and familiar faces. Before long, the baby responds with cooing sounds and can hold an object. Not yet six months old and the baby laughs... begins to sit... learns to stand. And, in the blink of an eye, a year has passed and your tiny, vulnerable baby is almost a toddler.

So much change packed into such a short period of time can make it hard to remember what happened when. This album is designed to help you record these important developments month by month for the first year of your child's life. It's something you'll treasure and, as your child gets older, he or she will enjoy looking at it with you.

Not only do children change a great deal in that first year, so do their parents. For many the birth of a child, especially the first child, is a life-changing event. It's not just lifestyle that changes but often our whole outlook on life. A child stirs powerful emotions: a love as profound as this is full of joy but also many fears. The quotations included in this album try to capture these feelings by giving expression to the spiritual dimension of becoming a family.

The famous words of the medieval Christian mystic, Julian of Norwich, serve as a consoling mantra for all new parents: 'All shall be well, and all shall be well, and all manner of things shall be well.'

Before you were born

You might like to use these pages to capture memories of life before your child was born! Perhaps you could include a picture of pregnant mum or the scan print.

The date you were due to be born . . . .

'When my bones were being formed, carefully put together in my mother's womb, when I was growing there in secret, you knew that I was there— you saw me before I was born.'

From Psalm 139

'Finally, I had a coherent thought, and that thought was: "I am not just me anymore. I am going to be someone's mother." And oh, it was magical and wonderful—and totally absurd.'

Arlene Matthews

The day you were born

This is a day which will provoke a mixture of memories, some you'll always treasure and some you'd rather forget! Here's space to record a few of them, including the first photos of your child.

Date of birth . . . .

Time . . . .

Place . . . .

'Here she is then… here, alive, the one
I must possess and guard. A year ago this
space was empty, not even a hope of her was
in it. Now she's here, brand new, with our
name upon her…'

Laurie Lee

Our newborn child

You might like to use these pages to record your first impressions of your baby. You could include early photographs and other memorabilia, such as the hospital name tag.

Full name . . . .

Birth weight . . . .

Length . . . .

Colour of eyes . . . .

Colour of hair . . . .

'May God be gracious to
us and bless us
and make his face to
shine upon us.'

From Psalm 67

'Twice or thrice had I loved thee,
Before I knew thy face or name.'

John Donne

Your first month

Changes, developments, experiences of this month:

....

....

....

....

....

....

....

....

....

Weight at the end of the first month ....

Your second month

Changes, developments, experiences of this month:

....

....

....

....

....

....

....

....

Weight at the end of the second month ....

Your third month

Changes, developments, experiences of this month:

....

....

....

....

....

....

....

....

Weight at the end of the third month ....

A special day

Whether it is a church
service to welcome
a child into God's
family, or a party for
family and friends, most
parents want some kind of
public celebration of their new arrival.
Here's space to record your child's special day.

'God is the creator of all things and by the birth of children he gives parents a share in the work and joy of creation.'

The Alternative Service Book 1980

Your fourth month

Changes, developments, experiences of this month:

....

....

....

....

....

....

....

....

....

Weight at the end of the fourth month ....

Your fifth month

Changes, developments, experiences of this month:

....

....

....

....

....

....

....

....

Weight at the end of the fifth month ....

Your sixth month

Changes, developments, experiences of this month:

....

....

....

....

....

....

....

....

Weight at the end of the sixth month ....

Special occasions and holidays

Here's space to record some of the special times together.

'Everything of the past and
everything of the present and
everything of the future God
creates in the innermost
realms of the soul.'
Meister Eckhart

'What do I remember, looking back? Beds made,
and shopping done? Housework finished and
work carried out efficiently? Not a bit of it. I
remember the odd unexpected moments...
moments spent by the pool, instead of hurrying
home from school; visits to the local park to see
the black sheep with curly horns...'
Kath Short

Your seventh month

Changes, developments, experiences of this month:

. . . .

. . . .

. . . .

. . . .

. . . .

. . . .

. . . .

. . . .

Weight at the end of the seventh month . . . .

Your eighth month

Changes, developments, experiences of this month:

....

....

....

....

....

....

....

....

Weight at the end of the eighth month ....

Your ninth month

Changes, developments, experiences of this month:

....

....

....

....

....

....

....

....

Weight at the end of the ninth month ....

Growth and development records

Upper teeth

Lower teeth

On this chart, number the teeth in the order they came through. Write the date when they appeared.

1 ....

2 ....

3 ....

4 ....

5 ....

6 ....

7 ....

8 ....

9 ....

10 ....

1 ....

2 ....

3 ....

4 ....

5 ....

6 ....

7 ....

8 ....

9 ....

10 ....

Height chart

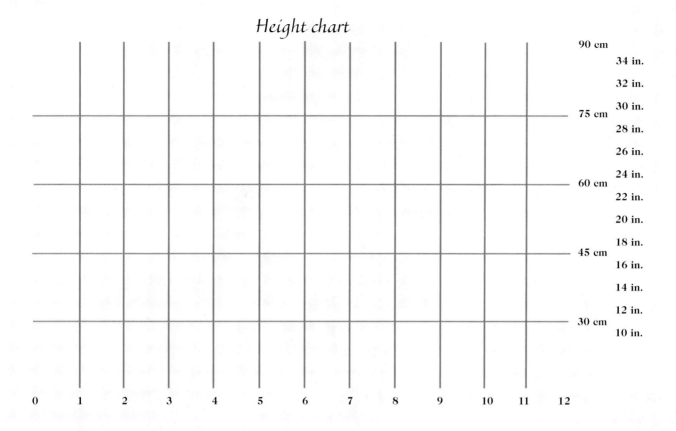

90 cm
34 in.
32 in.
30 in.   75 cm
28 in.
26 in.
24 in.   60 cm
22 in.
20 in.
18 in.   45 cm
16 in.
14 in.
12 in.   30 cm
10 in.

0 1 2 3 4 5 6 7 8 9 10 11 12

Weight chart

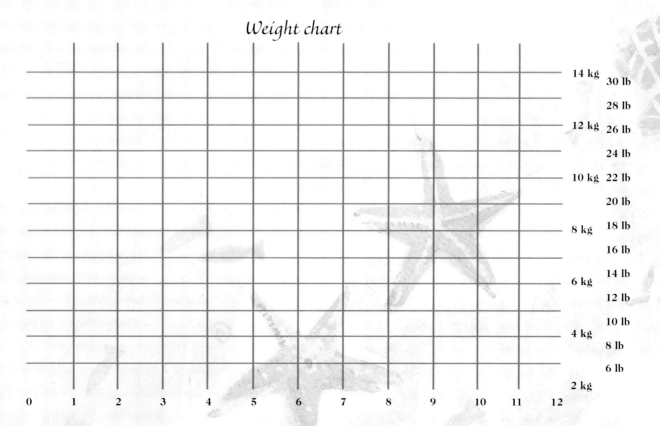

14 kg   30 lb
28 lb
12 kg   26 lb
24 lb
10 kg   22 lb
20 lb
8 kg   18 lb
16 lb
6 kg   14 lb
12 lb
10 lb
4 kg   8 lb
6 lb
2 kg

0 1 2 3 4 5 6 7 8 9 10 11 12

Your tenth month

Changes, developments, experiences of this month:

. . . .

. . . .

. . . .

. . . .

. . . .

. . . .

. . . .

. . . .

. . . .

Weight at the end of the tenth month . . . .

Your eleventh month

Changes, developments, experiences of this month:

....

....

....

....

....

....

....

....

....

Weight at the end of the eleventh month ....

Your twelfth month

Changes, developments, experiences of this month:

....

....

....

....

....

....

....

....

Weight at the end of the twelfth month ....

Happy first birthday!

It's hard to believe how quickly the first year goes by. Use these pages for photographs of your child's first birthday.

'Who is it that says most? Which can say more than this rich praise, that you alone are you?'
William Shakespeare

Milestones

Date

First outing . . . .

First smile . . . .

First slept through the night . . . .

First tooth . . . .

First solid food . . . .

First laugh . . . .

First 'swim' . . . .

First sat unsupported . . . .

First crawled . . . .

First pulled myself to standing . . . .

First steps . . . .

First word . . . .

First haircut . . . .

First pair of proper shoes . . . .

What a year!

first week

1 month old

2 months old

6 months old

7 months old

11 months old

3 months old

4 months old

5 months old

8 months old

9 months old

10 months old

12 months old

Family tree

Great-grandfather ....

Great-grandmother ....   Grandfather ....

Great-grandfather ....   Grandmother ....

Great-grandmother ....

Great-grandfather ....

Great-grandmother ....   Grandfather ....

Great-grandfather ....   Grandmother ....

Great-grandmother ....

Father ....

Mother ....

Our baby ....

*Children are a gift from the Lord;
they are a real blessing.*

From Psalm 127